OUT-SMARTING YOUR KARMA
And Other PreOrdained Conditions

OUT-SMARTING YOUR KARMA
And Other PreOrdained Conditions

BARRY NEIL KAUFMAN

Drawings by Laurie Campbell

EPIC CENTURY PUBLISHERS

OUT-SMARTING YOUR KARMA
And Other PreOrdained Conditions
Copyright © 1996 by Barry Neil Kaufman

Drawings by Laurie Campbell

Published by Epic Century Publishers,
a division of Epic Communications Corporation,
2080 South Undermountain Road, Sheffield, Massachusetts 01257-9643

Portions of this book reprinted from *The Book Of Wows And Ughs*
by Barry Neil Kaufman

Library of Congress Card Catalog Number 95-067841
ISBN # 1-887254-04-8
Cover design by Lightbourne Images, Copyright © 1996
Printed in the United States of America

A Special Dedication to Melissa Ford
who cherished the thoughts presented in this book and encouraged me to
see the power of transformation that could be contained in a "one-liner."
To her, my deepest gratitude and love.

Sometimes it is the simplest thought that allows us to cut through the clutter of confusion and, in a moment of time, reframe our beliefs and worldviews. The reflections and insights in this book are offered in the hope that they may gently and playfully tickle your mind to question your "reality"... and inspire you to recreate your thoughts (and therefore, your life) so that everyday experiences become more sensible, friendly, fulfilling and empowering.

HAPPY PEOPLE

Happy people
are loving.
Fearful people
are busy
with other
things.

1

ATTITUDINAL TRANSFORMATION

When everything
has changed
though nothing
is different.

CHOOSING

Choosing
is either
consenting
to our wants
or going
against
them.

BEYOND UNHAPPINESS

When unhappiness
is no longer
a question,
we are one.

WORLDVIEW

The difference
between
a flower
and a weed
is a judgment.

3

FORGIVENESS

We would not have
to forgive people
if we didn't judge them
in the first place.

4

THE LESSON

We thought ourselves
into unhappiness
by making judgments
...now we can think
ourselves back out
by letting them go.

REVELATION

What would happen
if our motto was
"I do not seek;
I find"?

STATE OF MIND

Unhappiness exists
either as a regret about the past
or a worry about the future.
The cure: be present.

FAIR

When I say,
"Life isn't fair,"
it means
I'm unhappy I'm the loser.
When I am the winner,
"fairness"
is not a question.

INTELLIGENCE

An intelligent person
doesn't have
to have
all the answers;
he just knows
where to go
to get them.

A BRIBE

A bribe
is an unhappy trade.

MEMORY

Yesterday
played back today
is no longer yesterday.
It's now.

WISDOM

Rather than judge,
try to understand.
Rather than push away,
try to embrace.
Rather than cling,
try to let go.
Eventually,
we can stop trying
and really do it.

UNLEARNING

Being myself
is a continual
process of
un-learning.

A WHOLE LIFE

Whether we live
a day,
a month,
or a hundred
years,
we have lived
a whole life.
A long life
never made living
good;
it just made it
long.

PROTOCOL

The secret
of happiness
is not in events
but in our responses
to them.

UNPREDICTABLE

Reasonable people
recreate the past;
unreasonable ones
recreate the world.

GIVING

Some of us
fear sharing
our love...
as if it comes
in limited editions.

FORGET

I can never
remember
what I didn't
want to hear
in the first
place.

DISCOVERY

Knowledge
cannot be found
under a rock.
Knowledge
is what we conclude
about what we see
under the rock.

TEACHER

A teacher
is not
a cup filler,
but a midwife
who helps
students
give birth
to themselves.

EDUCATION

Learning
is not a process
of being taught
what you don't
know
but the act
of discovering
how much
you do know.

RIPPLES ON THE POND

One more
happy person
on the planet
definitely
makes a difference.
What are you
waiting for?

UNFLINCHING OPTIMISM

Everyone is lovable.
Everyone can
express love.
One loving person,
one sincerely
loving person,
changes the world.

USEFUL DEFINITION

Loving people means
1) accepting them
2) wanting the best for them
3) being useful in helping
them get the best.

<u>FATE</u>

We talk about
falling in love
and falling down
the stairs
in the same way
...as if we're having
a colossal accident.

OUR GOOD-BYES

When I didn't get
unhappy about it,
they said I didn't care.
They mourned their loss
while I enjoyed
what I remembered.

THE BIG DIPPER

Psychoanalysis
is skin-diving
into a bathtub
of old bones
and broken
records.

PROMISE

A promise
is what
we tell each other
when we're not sure
we want to do it.

TO SONS
AND DAUGHTERS

My anger
says something
about me
and nothing
about you.

ANXIETY

Her hands
were so delicate that
when I touched them,
her fingers cracked.

DEAR OLD DAD

The pillar
and the rock,
the mountain
in the mist.
Dear old Dad
had a leather belt
he used
when he got pissed...
"A red ass never
forgets."

15

<u>REWARD</u>

Some people
put happiness
out there...
like the carrot
held in front of
a donkey.

EYES

I used to believe
I saw with my eyes.

CONNECTED

It was curious --
as she massaged
the bottom of my foot,
I noticed my eyes
relaxing.

SIMPLE

When I let myself
know how to do it,
I call it simple.

TOMORROW

Time floats
as they sail on their faces
into the future.

Planning,
fearing,
fantasizing
their tomorrows
today.

In effect,
they have no now,
leaving the future,
ironically, without
a past.

ADDICTION

We stare bug-eyed
at the eleven o'clock news,
striving to be well-informed,
as if knowledge
of the latest disasters
will enhance our sense
of well-being.

19

REVERENCE

In our prayers,
we tell God what to do.
Fix this. Heal that.
Change him. Change her.
As if we know better
than the intelligence
of the universe.
If we trusted God,
our prayers
would be more
like oceans
of gratitude
and poems
of love.

ALONE

Being alone
is just being alone.
Being lonely
is being unhappy
about being alone.

DISEMPOWERING BELIEFS

1) I can't get what I want.
2) There are limited possibilities.
3) The universe is hostile.

EMPOWERING BELIEFS

1) I can get what I want.
2) There are limitless possibilities.
3) The universe is friendly.

RELATIONSHIP TRIPPING

"If you loved me,
you would..."
(for example)
take the garbage out
every night
as proof.

I "need" you
to do what
I expect
so I can feel good
about myself
. . . maybe.

WIN-WIN

The real meaning
of "win-win"
in relationships:
not judging you
and not judging me.

BAROMETER

Feeling good
is my body's way
of experiencing
my happiness.

SHARING

Sharing
is allowing
you a place
in my space.

THE IDIOT

Someone
who is happy
all the time
is called
a happy idiot.
I see them
as being nice
to themselves.

BETWEEN THE LINES

Sometimes we say
something
and it lingers there
for years.
Sometimes
the "something"
never gets said
and yet has
even greater influence.

PASSIVITY

They peered around the corner,
saw it happen to everyone's dismay;
yet no one stirred or thought.
Conversing in old familiar tones,
a bystander whispered,
"Why doesn't
someone
do something?"

It's hard to break a habit.

PUSHING

When you
push someone,
they usually
push back.

Pushing is
standing still
or moving in the
opposite direction
from what you want.

GRIEF

I cried
all night
after you left;
otherwise,
how would I
know
I cared?

SACRED UNION

Some people
actually
have wars
in their beds.

AMPLIFICATION

By giving away
what we want most
(love, money, gratitude),
we create a
greater abundance of
the very commodity
we seek.
What goes around
comes around.

PROGRAMMING

"Garbage in,
garbage out."
Computer programmers
know that output
will always be
a function of input.
It works the same way
with food and
knowledge:
garbage in,
garbage out.

INTRODUCTION

We build
walls between us
and our enemies.
We construct
bridges between us
and our friends.
Isn't it time
to build more
bridges?

PUNISHMENT

Punishment
is the unhappy way
we ask others
to change
...often,
they kick us back.

PERSPECTIVES

"You can't look at life
through rose-colored glasses,"
they said, forgetting to add,
"...but it's perfectly okay
to see the world
through mud-brown lenses."

NATURE KNOWS

A photon of light
travels the path
of least resistance
(from the sun to the earth)
to arrive at its destination.
In physics, it's called
the principle of least action.
In human dynamics,
it's called "making it easy
for ourselves."
Making something hard
never makes it better
...it just makes it hard.

WORK

When we decide
to dislike
what we do,
we call it work.
Sometimes,
we call activities
we love "work"
and learn
to hate them.

LOVE LASTS

Once we take charge
of being loving,
we can fuel
that experience
with every breath,
even when others
don't return our caring.
Then, truly,
our love will last.

CONGRUENCY

When I
am happy,
what I want
for my lover
is precisely
what she wants
for herself.

ALONE

Even as we love
one another,
what she does
is for her
and what I do
is for me.
Each of us
is alone
with our choices.

LOVE

To love someone
is to be
happy with
who and what
they are,
accepting them
without
conditions.

SORROW

It lasted all morning,
the mourning;
tears dripped from her face...
until someone asked,
"Do you want a hot fudge
ice cream sundae
with whipped cream?"
Then she smiled.

GREAT EXPECTATIONS

"When can I go
into the supermarket
and buy what I want
with my good looks?"
Allen Ginsberg asked
many years ago.
Some things
haven't changed.

WANTING

We
either
go with
our wanting
or against it.
Either way,
we do
what we're
wanting.

MAYBE

Maybe,
perhaps,
perchance...
that's my way
of deciding
not to
decide.

THE ULTIMATE
ROMANCE

Love is a choice,
which means
I don't have to wait
for a chemical reaction
or years of bonding
to give myself
that feeling.
I can choose to
love you right now!

AUTHENTICITY

Honesty
is not a license
to kill...
it's an opportunity
to share more
of who you are.

CANDID

You announce
your honesty
up front
so everyone
can prepare
themselves
for the lie.

SMOKE SCREEN

"Collateral damage"
might sound
like walking
on lawns and shrubs,
but military folks
use this expression
to describe
killing civilians.
"Peacemakers"
refer to MX missiles.
We sure have
a way with words,
especially when
we're trying to make
an impression.

37

HITTING

A child
doesn't remember
the lesson,
only the aggression...
try hitting
a brick wall
next time.

INFANT

Her tiny
hands
opened
to catch
you and me.
Were we
there?

DEAF EARS

"Don't listen
to my tone of voice, pal,
just hear the content
of what I say."
Of course, these words
also fell on deaf ears.

THIEF

The robber
only robs
what wasn't
yours...
how can he
steal you
from you?

EXPECTATION

When I expect
to get something,
I stop wanting it
and begin needing it
in order to be
happy.

ME

I only observe myself
when I stop
and then I'm not.
This dilemma
was solved when
I allowed myself to be,
and that was me
...unobserved.

ME AND GOD

Without
eye shadow,
rouge
or lipstick,
she looked into
the mirror
and faced
her face:
"God and I agree;
this is the
way I am."

MOUTH

My way in
as well as
my way out...
my mouth.

MEDIATION

Negotiation
is much more
useful than
self-righteousness.

THE GIVER GETS

In order to love someone,
we have to fill ourselves
with love.
Loving others
is not a selfless sacrifice
but a fulfilling
of who we are
and what we want.

DELIVERANCE

Believe in yourself
and your dreams.
Look for possibilities,
not limits.
Deliver acceptance
instead of judgment,
love instead of hate.

42

ASSUMPTIONS

We all have
blind spots
but no holes
appear in
our visual field.
The brain fills
in the spaces
with the best guess
as to what might
actually be there.
What we see
is not really there.
We do the same
with our assumptions,
believing we know
what people
think and feel
without ever asking.

What would happen
if we asked?

HEALING PARADOX

The more
you give love,
the more love
you have to give.

LETHAL EMOTIONS

Drive-by shootings,
child abuse,
and rape are
visible eruptions
of the unhappiness
in our hearts.
When a group of us
do unhappiness together,
that's called war.

The antidote:
teach happiness,
teach love.

MIND BENDER

Know the truth
and it will
set you free...
and there is
no truth.

ALLOWING

You don't
work at
being happier;
you allow it.

GHOST

The electrode
showed the brain
had initiated the action
0.35 seconds before
the person had
the intention to act.
Who's in charge here,
anyway?

CYBERSPACE

Anywhere,
everywhere,
even here.
Today...
information,
tomorrow...
simulation
of you and me.
We are beginning
to have
our out-of-body
experiences
on the keyboard.

REFLECTIONS

In the mirror,
I've never seen
more than
my skin.

ETERNITY

I have never met
a man who believed
he could live forever.
I guess that's why
nobody has.

MENTOR

You were there
when I wanted you
...never needing me
to need you.
You smiled when I
screamed,
I remember.

47

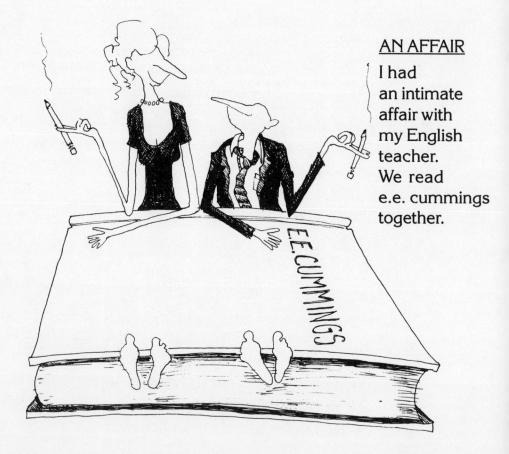

AN AFFAIR

I had
an intimate
affair with
my English
teacher.
We read
e.e. cummings
together.

PILGRIMAGE

When I was unhappy,
I met an angry God.
When I became happier,
I met an accepting God.
And when I learned to love,
I met a loving God.
We find what we
want to find.

DIVIDEND

Why would we
want to believe
that we can change
ourselves
quickly, easily
and without pain?
Because beliefs
become
self-fulfilling
prophecies.

BREATH

Breathing.
It sustains us,
feeds our bodies
and our minds.
An effortless action
performed 23,040 times
each day.
Sit back, relax
and take another
breath.
Isn't life awesome?

CORRELATION

I notice
the happier I am,
the more loving
I am.
It was nice
to notice that.

UN-HEALTH

"Dis-eased"
means
not-at-ease,
not comfortable,
away from
the natural flow.
What a
clear definition
of unhappiness!

HEALTH

Health is not
a question
when you have it
but becomes one
when you don't.

PATIENT

Some people
see disease
as their enemy...
they ask others
to wage war
against their
illnesses,
making
battlefields of
their bodies.

52

MEDICINE

The medication
beat the disease
and the patient
to death,
all at the same
time.

REGENERATION

Medicine
and surgery
can never be
a substitute
for the real
healing agent
in your system
...you.

OPENING
THE HEART

People
who open
their hearts
and minds
to everyone
are often called
saints.
I call them
smart.

POWERHOUSE

"You make me
angry."
Message:
"You control
how I feel."

PRIDE

"I know better
than you."
Message:
"You're not
smart enough
to know."

ACCUSATION

"Can't you
get it right?"
Message:
"Something is
wrong with you."

ABSENCE

"Take your medicine
or you won't get better."
Message:
"Only intervention
from outside
can heal you."

COMMANDMENT

"Be seen,
not heard."
Message:
"What you say
doesn't matter."

UNSUBSTANTIATED

"You're too young
to understand."
Message:
"When you
get older,
you'll get smarter."

BLINDFOLD

"Stop asking
so many questions."
Message:
"Understanding
is not important."

55

SETTING THE STAGE

"I can't anticipate
being healthy
forever."
Message:
"I have no control;
disease is inevitable."

GUIDANCE

The only healing
that ever takes place
is self-healing.
Medications
and massages
just encourage
your body
to do what
it knows to do.

PRESCRIPTION

"A merry heart
doeth thee good
like medicine."
Even the scriptures
gave us
permission
to be happy
and healthy.
What are we
waiting for?

PAIN

If your body
quietly crept up
upon your head,
kicked you in the face
and left you for dead,
would you call it a sign?

PRONOID

Some depressed people
are diagnosed
as paranoid.
Now doctors
are labeling happy folks
as pronoid,
a new category
of mental disorder
of the "pleasant type."
Symptoms can be
optimism, joy and
a super self-image.
Contentment would be
a milder form
of this illness.
Humm...happiness
now comes with
a warning label.

ON BEING HUMAN

They say
feeling bad is
only human...
but I like
to celebrate my
humanity,
not with my
unhappiness,
but with my loving
and caring.

PROGRAMMED UNHAPPINESS

Guilt is what
a "good" person
believes
she should feel
when she has done
something "bad."

GUILT

Another name
for paying
your dues.

THE ONLY PARADIGM

The way we choose
to see the world
creates the world
we see.

BEAUTY

Although the
others
saw it as ugly,
when I decided
it was beautiful,
it truly was.

EXPLANATIONS

The law of gravity
doesn't exist
"out there."
It's a conclusion
existing in our heads
about what's
"out there."

THE PATH

In this universe
of curved space,
a light beam
sent out in any direction
will eventually find
its way back
to the source.
God's waiting
for us.

VOICES

A loud voice
cannot compete
with a clear
voice,
even if it's
a whisper.

DIGITIZED I

They look
like multilegged bugs,
little silicon chips
with microscopically
tiny electronic switches.
They direct flashes
of electricity
moving at blinding speeds.
They do functions
a million times faster
than the human beings
who designed them.
They are our creations,
as much a part of nature
as the oak tree.

DIGITIZED II

Social mobility
now covers the
planet.
The digerati surf
along copper wires
and fiber-optic
cables
seeking solace
in cyberspace.
Information rules,
but pornography
and the personals
still lure those
seeking to be
touched.

AFTER ALL THESE YEARS

One fiber-optic line
could deliver a million
cable channels
of television
concurrently.
We can compress,
encode and decode
images and sounds
with dazzling perfection.
We have become
electronic wizards,
informing, distracting
and entertaining.
And yet we can't
figure out how not
to be bored
when we are alone
and how not
to be frustrated
when we don't get
our way.

FORTUNE TELLING

"If I don't
get the promotion,
I will be heartbroken."
"If she leaves me,
I will be heartbroken."
We promise
ourselves now
to be miserable later.
Isn't it amazing
how we can
predict the future?

BOTTOM LINE QUESTION

"Is this good for me
or bad for me?"
The "good for me"
answer
results in hope
and happiness.
The "bad for me"
response
brings distress
and discomfort.
It's our choice.

EVIL

When we fear
something,
we give it
horns and a tail.

BLINDERS

If I look
only for what
I expect to see,
I'll miss
all the other
flowers
in the garden.

DEEP

When we don't understand
and don't want to say
we don't understand...
we pass it off
as deep.

I.Q.

There are
no stupid people
in the world,
just unhappy ones.

TENDING TOWARD

Wanting
is already
moving toward
something.

ABSTRACTIONS

People who get
killed in wars
or starve
to death
are "them,
over there,"
never you or I.

MAKE BELIEVE

We create myths
to explain
what we don't
understand.
Sometimes,
we call our myths
facts.

INTROVERT

Closing me "in"
is very different
from closing you "out"...
although the appearances
are similar.

HARMONY

Harmony
is two or more
people
smiling
at each other.

DISSONANCE

Dissonance
is when
two people
hit the same note
at the same time
and there is only
room for one.

A GROUP

A group
is many people
making believe
they're
together.

TIME WARP

If the sun exploded,
we would not be aware
of the event for eight
minutes.
Our "present" would
be suspended
between a fictitious past
(the sun is intact)
and a hypothetical future
(the sun has exploded).
The lesson:
the only real game
in town
is the present
moment.

THROUGH THE YEARS

At the age of thirty,
we have 245 taste buds.
By the time we are eighty,
only 88 are left.
Yet life can grow
sweet as we age
if we use the years
to love more,
appreciate more
and let go.

THE C.E.O.

Each of us
has six hundred
voluntary muscles
that we can maneuver
consciously.
Our bodies change
biochemically
every time we alter
our thoughts.
How can we ever say
we are out of control?

BODY CONTACT

The skin
of a six-foot man
would make, if spread out,
a 4 x 5 foot area rug.
The lungs of the same man,
if unfolded and spread out,
would cover a room
32 x 2l feet.
Our lungs, taking in
breath after breath,
are the organs
that have the greatest
amount of contact
with the outside world.
Even deep inside
our bodies,
we are married
to the universe
around us.
We are neither separate
nor alone.

ROLE MODEL

He held his fist high,
protesting the war.
With anger in his heart
and unspoken judgments
on his lips,
he lobbied for peace,
never realizing
he was part
of the violence.

THE PATH

Whether
we go "forward"
or move "backwards,"
we're always
on our way.

SELF-FULFILLING PROPHECY

I always
wanted to sing,
but I have
a terrible
voice.

MASQUERADE

Ninety-eight percent
of the atoms
in our bodies
are replaced
each year in
a continuous process
of death and birth.
Since we are born anew
in every second,
we can stop
pretending to be fossils,
as if our opinions
and behaviors
were carved in granite
and not changeable.

FEARS

Usually we
retreat from
our fears
or we assault them.
These activities are
different from
dispensing
with them.

ESCAPE

He always
found himself
falling asleep
at the best
parts.

A DRIVE IN THE COUNTRY

Cars and relationships
have some things
in common.
Both have accelerators
and brakes.
So if your partnership
is out of control or stalled,
check out where you
are putting your feet.

METAPHOR

Those who live
metaphorically,
deserve a punch
in a rose.

NO ESCAPE

They drink
together
to get together,
but somehow
they're even
further apart.

HOLY MISSION

We rush
into the
supermarkets
to buy our boxes
of doughnuts,
only to arrive
home,
moaning
and groaning
about the holes
in the doughnuts.

PUMP

An illusion,
a glass of wine
and a friend —
often we think
we have to keep
filling them up
in order to get
what we want.

LABELS

When my hands
tingle before
a test,
I call it fear.
When my hands
tingle
before sex,
I call it
excitement.
Hmmmm.

FAT LOGIC

Moving
from the pantry
to the stove,
I noticed
I wasn't hungry
...so I proceeded
to eat.

REALITY CHECK

To his child
he said,
"I hit you because
I love you."
Correction:
"I hit you because
I am angry."
When we are
doing anger,
we are not doing love.

MANIPULATION

I don't know
why he calls me
a control freak.
I just want
my way.

DESTINY

Some of us
create the future;
some of us
just let it happen.
Others turn around
and wonder,
"What happened?"

TRANSFER
STATION

Our pop culture
dumps carloads
of expectations
at the doorstep
of every adolescent.

THE LOSING HAND

"No pain, no gain."
"Life is a constant struggle."
"You never really get
what you want."
"There is no justice."
"No one cares."
And, of course,
"Something is wrong
with you."
Hold these beliefs
and there is no reason
to get out of bed
in the morning.

THE FLOW

When
Beethoven
turned deaf
in a slow,
subtle manner
and the doctors
coughed their
question marks,
no one understood
except the ol' boy.
He knew the rhythm;
he had spent
his whole life
composing it,
conducting it,
and he also knew
the rhythm of time
he could not
direct.

GIFT

What we get
on our birthday
is a present.
A gift
comes unexpected
and without
wrapping paper,
like a smile.

PERSON TO PERSON

The best
I can do
is to tap
your awareness
of what you
already know.

A QUESTION

A question
can be a statement,
a disguised
accusation,
or simply
an opportunity
to bring
what you "know"
to life.

TRANSFORMATION

The old question:
What's possible?
The new question:
What do I want?
The old question
is about the past.
The new question
is about the future.

NURTURING BIAS

Deciding:
everything happens
for everyone's
benefit.
Sometimes, we're
too shortsighted
to grasp
all the benefits.

If God is good,
then this bias
makes good sense.

RIVER OF LIFE

We can never put
our foot into the river
in the same place twice.
In every millisecond
the water changes,
as does the river of blood
inside our leg.
Life celebrates itself
by endless movement
and change.
No reason to cling
or to hold on.
Our job is to go
with the current
and let it lift us free.
In this universe, nothing dies.
We are matter.
We become energy,
then matter and energy again.
We are in the river and of the river,
constantly reborn.

TOGETHER

My daughter
once asked me
why people have only
five fingers on each hand.
I told her I don't know.
We were very close
that morning.

SILENCE

The spaces
between our words
are often
more profound
than the chatter
...silence is
another way
to be together.

PRELUDE

Butter melts
better on hot toast;
that's why
she kissed him
before they went
to bed.

THE MIND

I used to believe
my best thinking
was done in my brain
until I stubbed
my big toe.

PARADISE

It is said
that heaven
is not so much
a location
as a state of mind.
We live
in paradise
but cannot see it.
Instead,
we make up
hell
in place of
heaven.

NAIVE

No one
ever loses
their innocence;
they just
change their
attitude.

ENTERTAIN

She entertains me,
which means
she keeps
her distance.

SHOWBOAT

He flexes his muscles
and pushes out his chest.
He tightens his stomach
and says he's the best.
He's coming on...
or so he thinks.

Pass the pretzels.

BIOSPHERE

Gravity
is our way
of explaining
why we're stuck.
How convenient!

ILLUSIONS

We don't see
the Andromeda galaxy
in our telescopes.
We see light
and the reflection
of two million years ago.
What is...
isn't, really.

SELF-ACCEPTANCE

Knowing that
anything
we learn
about ourselves
can only be...
beautiful
and useful.

SURGERY

Remove
the suffering
and you
get happiness.

CHAOS

You're
confused!
How wonderful.
You've taken
a giant step
towards
enlightenment.

ANIMAL

An animal moves
by instinct
and intuition,
while you and I
often stumble over
our thoughts.

SWITCH-HITTER

I call my stomach
my belly
when it's full.
I call my belly
my stomach
when it's ill
...or empty.

WALLFLOWER

A person
who waits on
the sidelines
for someone
to jingle
his gonads.

AWARE

As he eats
the chocolate cake,
he says he wants
to go on a diet.

If you want
to know
what people
really want,
ignore their words;
watch what
they do.

DEAD END

A hateful
person
lives in
a hateful
world.

EMPTY CUP

When he says
he is trying,
it means
he's not delivering.

94

BEGGARS

We walk around
like panhandlers,
asking others
to fill our cups
with love
so we can feel
good.

GENESIS

When we say
we've changed
our minds,
we make
a statement
of fact.
Our minds
and bodies
change
electromagnetically,
biochemically
and structurally
each time
we change
a belief.

Welcome
to creation
and evolution.

CHANGING PRIORITIES

Is the pursuit
of happiness and love
a meaningful endeavor
or just self-indulgence?
What impact would
a happy, loving
head of state
have on a nation,
a happy, loving
general
have on an army,
a happy, loving
doctor
have on a patient,
a happy, loving
teacher
have on a student
a happy, loving
parent
have on a child?
You decide.

GRAND ILLUSION #1

Unhappiness is
a natural, unavoidable
characteristic
of the human condition.

GRAND ILLUSION #2

Unhappiness is
the result of certain beliefs
which we have adopted
and which we can change.

GRAND ILLUSION #3

We have a choice.
We can believe
Illusion #1 or #2.

CONFUSION

The more
I thought
about it,
the less
I seemed
to know...
as if my thoughts
kept getting
in my way.

APPEARANCE

Doing something
for you
is doing something
for me
...that's why
I do it.

COMPARISONS

The little boy
looked sheepishly
at his glass
half empty;
he called it ugly.
When she refilled it
to the top
with juice,
he smiled
and called it
beautiful...
even little children
talk in metaphors.

CLIENT

"Client"
is a fancy way
of saying,
"He gives
me money."

HAPPY PEOPLE

Happy people
always get
what they want
or want
what they get.

DISAPPROVAL

If I disapprove
of my headache,
it seems to linger...
but when I go
with it,
the pain passes
quickly.

ON BECOMING A FORCE OF NATURE

- Clarity of Purpose *(decide to make a difference)*
- Conviction *(believe in what you're about to do)*
- Daring *(stand tall even in the face of opposition)*
- Passion *(once committed, give it all you've got)*
- Persistence *(stay the race until the end)*

When you become a "force of nature,"
there are never any regrets.
Giving so deeply and fully is its own reward.

CHILDREN

Little people
who have civil rights
are called midgets;
the other little people
who do not have
civil rights
are called children.

CRY

A baby's cry
isn't unhappy
until someone
judges it to be.

FAMINE

Feed just one
starving person
a sandwich or
an apple
and you change
the face of
starvation
on the planet.

POLLUTION

The rivers
are called
polluted
since they've
turned brown...
before that
the garbage didn't
offend us.

BEING TOUCHED

The only walls
we build
between us
are for
self-protection,
as if we had
to hide,
pretending
we didn't want
to be touched.

ONE PERSON'S "VISION TO LIVE BY"

- Go for what you want...in spite of the evidence.
- Remove the muzzle and be authentically YOU.
- Approach every "problem" as an opportunity.
- Make your enemies your friends.
- Know that you're doing the best you can (for now).
- Recognize that you're enough.
- Express gratitude by giving fully and freely.
- Invite into your life only what you really want.
- Live as if there are no wrong moves.
- Choose beliefs that lead to happiness, love and God.
- Encourage the miraculous by believing in the "impossible."

RESPONSIBILITY

I used to think
I caused
her unhappiness
until she complained
about my big nose;
then I left.

THINKING

Reasons
do not clarify
my wants;
they only support
my doubts.

PRIDE

"When I approve
of what my child does,
she's a reflection of me.
When I don't approve,
she's someone else's kid."

BIG MAKE-BELIEFS

"I didn't mean
to do it"...
and "I'll love you
forever."

CONCLUSIONS

The more
fire trucks
there are
at a fire,
the more people
seem to die.
Conclusion:
fire trucks
kill people.

RATIONALE

I need a reason
to hang out —
it's my way
of giving myself
permission to do
what I want.

CHECK-UP

Have you ever
wanted a tree house
over a cesspool
in the desert?
Well, neither
have I...
so now we can
both relax;
there's nothing wrong
with us.

FREE

If my happiness
never depended
on getting
what I said
I wanted,
then I could freely
want everything
...without getting
unhappy.

TRAIL BLAZER

All dreams appear
impossible
until someone
makes them happen.

PERMISSION

Carefully collecting
all the evidence
piece by piece,
we now decide.
Sure, it's arbitrary
but what else is
there to do?

DREAMING

If I were aware
of what I knew,
I might allow it...
so, instead, to be safe,
I experiment
in my dreams,
making everything
not what it seems.

LOVER TO LOVER

"It is all
arranged," he said.
"If you feel bad
when I feel bad,
then I will
feel better."

OPPOSITES

When we fight
our fears,
we give them
power.

PERMITTING

When I didn't
seem to know
which way
to turn,
I just followed
my body.

ENTRANCE

We can
either wait
to find a doorway
or make one...
it's your move.

ACCEPTABLE LIES

Research shows
that people tend
to believe praise
and like those
who provide it,
even when
the praise
is clearly false.
Lying to each other
seems to satisfy
our need
for approval,
but it also builds
walls of dishonesty
between us.

UNHAPPINESS

Unhappiness
is the queen
of our culture:
We fear death
in order to live,
punish in order
to prevent.

CHOICE

Every time
we deny it,
we do it
...we make
a choice.

LANGUAGE

We climb
a ladder of words
to our brain,
as if we
were not there.

STATISTICS

People love
to the extent
they are happy.

EVIDENCE

We use
the rules
as our tools
to gather
evidence.
That's because
we don't trust
what we know.

JUDGING

When
we can't
accept it,
we judge it.

ON BECOMING AN ADULT

As a child
I learned to pretend
to be unhappy
because it moved people.
Unhappiness got me
things.
Then I pretended
to be unhappy
because it moved me.
Finally, after
so much practice,
I forgot that
I was pretending.

On that day,
my childhood
escaped me.
I became an adult,
which means I often forget
to remember
I am only pretending.

SHOULD #1

When I believe
I "have to,"
"should" or "must"
go somewhere,
I usually want
to move in
the opposite
direction.

SHOULD #2

When I say
I should,
I am twisting
my arm
in the direction
it really wants
to go.

EQUATION

Misery
used to fight
misery
creates more
misery.

PREJUDICE

A label
is your way
of putting
distance
between you
and me.

DISTRUST

Sometimes
we feel bad
when we feel good
in order to stop ourselves.
Otherwise,
we might be good
to ourselves again
for no reason.

MISUSE

Angry
commentaries
are not signs
of authenticity;
they are signs
of anger.

MENU

We want
what we want
(money, sex,
friendship)
so we can,
in the end,
feel good.
Why not
make the dessert
the whole
meal?

TOMORROW

Worrying
about the future
is like trying
to eat the hole
in the doughnut.
It's munching
on what isn't.

COMING AND GOING

99.9% of all species
that lived on earth
are now extinct.
Yet, as species
go out of existence,
new ones come in.
Life celebrates itself
with an endless tide
of comings and goings.
No need to hang on,
no need to keep clinging.
Each ending
welcomes
a new beginning.

We can let go!

DECISIONS

The decision
to be happy
is actually
the decision
to stop
being unhappy.

WORDS

Sometimes
I begin to
believe my words
and lose sight
of myself.

A PROBLEM

It's only
a problem
as long as
I call it
a problem.

Problems
can be
welcomed
opportunities,
pregnant
with
solutions.

Reality
follows my
point-of-view.

REWRITE

"Forget the past
and you will
be doomed
to repeat it."
Rewrite:
"Stay present
and be happy
and you'll have
no reason
to remember
or repeat
the past."

THE BIG FLOP

Some scientists
believe that
a big crunch
will eventually
follow the big bang
of creation,
leaving nothing
in its wake.
They anticipate
the ultimate
black hole
from which
nothing
can escape,
not even God.
I wonder
if their beliefs
give them
warm fuzzies
at night?

PARTY

Rotting
in a corner
is not
taking
care of
yourself....
welcome
to the party.

PASSION

Six couples
eating ice cream
sundaes
with their shoes
off.

HEART AEROBICS

What we focus on
we make bigger,
like working muscles
with free weights
or blowing up
a tire with air.
Let's focus on
loving one another.

TIME

A beautiful woman
is like a rare
bottle of wine.
They're both aged,
only the woman says
she doesn't like it.

"MAKE"

I can't "make"
you unhappy;
only you
can do that,
you lucky dog.

CAUSE

I used
to look in the past
for the cause
of what I do,
but lately
I'm finding it
in the future.

DISGUISE

Calling it tragic
is my way
of saying
I'm afraid.

TRUTH OR DARE

Some helping professionals
argue that happiness
and truth are antagonists.
The evidence:
happy people believe
others like them and
think events will
work out to their benefit.
Depressed people
believe others don't like them
and anticipate bad things
happening.
The good doctors conclude
that depressed people,
though sadder,
are more accurate
and, thus, wiser!

Given this logic,
I'd trade wisdom
for happiness any time!

THE CHICKEN
OR THE EGG

Do we base
our beliefs
on the evidence
or does the evidence
follow from our beliefs?

FINGER POINTING

"She made me angry."
"He got me upset."
"They make me
frustrated."
When I blame you
for my feelings,
I make myself
a victim.
When I take
ownership
for my reactions,
I create opportunities
for change.

MOTIVATION

Every time we allow
someone to move us
with anger,
we teach them
to be angry.

IRRATIONAL

We can be
happy without
having a reason
...happiness
is reason enough.

CREATION

Every thought
is a physical event.
When we say we've
changed our mind,
we're not kidding.

KNOWING

How will I know
when I know?
When I have
no more questions.

DEATH

We kiss it
and curse it,
but always
at arm's length.

EFFECTIVENESS

Being effective
has nothing to do
with what we did,
but everything to do
with how we did it.

IDENTITY

Do not fold,
spindle or mutilate;
the hole in the card
is really me.

INTOLERANCE

Wanting
leads to
allowing;
needing
leads to
intolerance.

DEPRIVATION

I claimed
I denied myself
for you,
which just meant
I did exactly
what I wanted.

GAMES

I only
play games
when I'm
afraid
to be me.

CHEAP

Being cheap
is a dynamic
of cheating
yourself.

DENIAL

Saying
you want
to feel good
is denying
that you do.

DECISIONS

Your decisions
are not like
one-way streets...
even while
in the middle,
you can always
turn around.

<u>INFINITY</u>

Opportunity
knocks
so many times
it has
raw knuckles.

LOSING TOUCH

When I attend
to my fears
and discomforts,
it seems as if
I no longer know
what I'm wanting.

SETTLING DOWN

When he graduated
from college,
he settled down
to name-plated doors
and profit-sharing.

DEMOCRACY

Celebrities
take the reins
of government,
promising stardom
for everyone —
and autographs.

CEASE-FIRE

The streets filled
with angry, animated characters,
banded together aggressively,
an activated group.

Posters marked their cause,
their cry, their outrage.
Real people
breaking the communal habit,
speaking in loud, loud voices.

The eyes of an entire nation
watched them, hypnotized
by their own curiosity and concern.

Inevitably, the streets emptied.
Neighborhood bars filled
with opposing demonstrators
Two enemies of the day
tipped their mugs toward each other
and shared a smile.

FIREWORKS

Thoughts are
physical events
in our bodies,
experienced
as sensations
called emotions.
In effect,
we sensationalize
our thoughts.

Deciding to be grateful
generates a much sweeter sensation
than taking you for granted.

Deciding to love you
stimulates a much cozier sensation
than being neutral about
your presence.

We're in charge
of the fireworks
we call our feelings.

NEW WORLD

Happiness
is a choice
and misery
is optional,
not inevitable.

Imagine
if everyone
knew that.

Happiness Is A Choice: Presents a simple blueprint not only to empower the decision to be happy (create more inner ease, comfort and peace of mind) but also shares six shortcuts to happiness, each of which opens a doorway into an open-hearted state of mind. Contains the best of twenty-five years' experience working with tens of thousands of people - synthesized into an easily traveled, step-by-step journey to self-acceptance and empowerment. Published by Fawcett Columbine (Ballantine Books/Random House).

Son-Rise: The Miracle Continues: The original best-seller, ***Son-Rise***, made into an award-winning NBC special, has been viewed by 300 million people worldwide. This book not only presents the updated journal of Barry and Samahria Kaufman's successful efforts to reach their "unreachable" autistic son and heal him, but goes beyond to include the inspiring stories of five other families who used the same loving approach to heal their own very special children. Published by H.J. Kramer, Inc.

To Love Is To Be Happy With: Details the practical and powerful Option Process® and shows the reader how to use a simple dialogue format to replace beliefs which inhibit us with beliefs which will liberate us to be happy, loving and empowered. The cornerstone book of the Option Process® and manual to help people redesign their attitudes and lives. Published by Fawcett Crest (Ballantine Books/Random House).

Giant Steps: Presents ten intimate, uplifting, in-depth portraits of young people engaged in transformative dialogues with Kaufman and shows the mentoring process in action. The reader holds hands with young people who learn to break through their pain and triumph in the face of challenge and crisis. Published by Fawcett Crest (Ballantine Books/Random House).

A Miracle to Believe In: Shares a revealing portrait of Barry and Samahria Kaufman's working and healing lifestyle before they established their world-renowned learning center. This book gives an in-depth picture of their family and the group of daring volunteers who came together to love a special child back to life. Published by Fawcett Crest (Ballantine Books/Random House).

FutureSight: A psychic odyssey that will make you think twice before dismissing your next hunch or premonition. This gripping story details the journey of one couple whose relationship and destiny are forever changed by a series of haunting premonitions that not only threaten their lives but challenge them to find a deep and abiding level of self-trust. Published by Epic Century Publishers.

A Sacred Dying: This moving account of death's transcendence through love serves as an inspiration and guide for anyone dealing with the approaching death of someone who is loved or cherished. Additionally: a valuable resource and learning tool for therapists. It is the story of one family that learns to go beyond the pain and find a new way to celebrate life and each other. Published by Epic Century Publishers.

These books are available at local bookstores and libraries and also can be ordered by mail through Option Indigo Press. *Special Sales: All books available at special quantity discounts for organizations, premiums, fund-raising and educational use.*

Audiotapes include *The 12 Tape Option Process® Lecture Series, The Keys to Option Mentoring, Body Vital/Stress-Free Living, The Empowered Leader, No Fault/No Risk Parenting* — all by Barry Neil Kaufman, *Special Children/Special Solutions* by Samahria Lyte Kaufman. Videotapes include *Beyond the Limits* with Barry Neil Kaufman, *New Eyes-New Life, The Miracle of Love* and others. All audiotapes and videotapes, as well as all of the above books can be ordered by mail. For a free catalog and ordering information call or write:

Option Indigo Press, 2080 S. Undermountain Road
Sheffield, MA 01257-9643 (**1-800-562-7171**)

About the Author

Barry Neil Kaufman, along with his wife, Samahria Lyte Kaufman, teaches a uniquely self-accepting and empowering process (Option Process®) that also has educational and therapeutic applications. They are co-founders/co-directors of The Option Institute and Fellowship, (P.O.Box 1180-OK, 2080 South Undermountain Road, Sheffield, MA 01257-9643, 413-229-2100). The Institute offers personal growth workshops for individuals, couples, families and groups as well as individual counseling services. Workshops range from week-end and week-long exploratory sessions to eight week intensives. Custom designed corporate training programs for businesses and specialized seminars for helping professionals are also available. In the years since its founding, The Option Institute has served as a beacon of hope and possibility for thousands of people from across the United States as well as for individuals from many other countries.

Additionally, the Kaufmans present motivational talks at conferences, guide workshops and seminars, lecture at universities and appear in mass media throughout the country. As a result of their innovative and successful Son-Rise Program®, which they developed for their once-autistic son, the Kaufmans also counsel and instruct families wanting to create home-based, child-centered teaching programs for their own special needs children.

Mr. Kaufman has written ten books and coauthored two screenplays with his wife (winning the Christopher Award twice and the Humanitas Prize). In his landmark book, *Happiness Is A Choice,* he pulls together the best of over twenty-five years' experience working with thousands of individuals, and presents a blueprint of simple, concrete methods to empower the decision to be happy.

His first book, *Son-Rise,* which details his family's inspiring journey to heal their once-autistic child, was dramatized as an NBC television movie. His subsequent books include *Giant Steps, To Love Is To Be Happy With, A Miracle To Believe In, The Book Of Wows And Ughs!, A Sacred Dying, FutureSight* and *Son-Rise: The Miracle Continues.*

**For more information about the Option Institute call
1-800-71-HAPPY (1-800-714-2779)**